Hunting with HYENAS

By Kennon O'Mara

Gareth Stevens
Publishing

Please visit our website, www.garethstevens.com. For a free color catalog of all our high-quality books, call toll free 1-800-542-2595 or fax 1-877-542-2596.

Library of Congress Cataloging-in-Publication Data

O'Mara, Kennon.
Hunting with hyenas / by Kennon O'Mara.
 p. cm. — (Animal attack)
Includes index.
ISBN 978-1-4824-0493-7 (pbk.)
ISBN 978-1-4824-0492-0 (6-pack)
ISBN 978-1-4824-0494-4 (library binding)
1. Hyenas — Juvenile literature. I. Title.
QL737.C24 O43 2014
599.743—dc23

First Edition

Published in 2014 by
Gareth Stevens Publishing
111 East 14th Street, Suite 349
New York, NY 10003

Copyright © 2014 Gareth Stevens Publishing

Designer: Katelyn E. Reynolds
Editor: Therese Shea

Photo credits: Cover, p. 1 (cover, pp. 1, 3–24 background image) Mary Beth Angelo/Photo Researchers/Getty Images; cover, pp. 1, 3–24 (background graphic) pashabo/Shutterstock.com; cover, pp. 4–23 (splatter graphic) jgl247/Shutterstock.com; pp. 5, 7 (brown hyena), 15, 19 iStockphoto/Thinkstock.com; pp. 6, 11, 14, 20 Hemera/Thinkstock.com; p. 7 (spotted hyena) Fuse/Thinkstock.com; p. 9 Peter Schwarz/Shutterstock.com; p. 12 Anton_Ivanov/Shutterstock.com; p. 13 Daniel Alvarez/Shutterstock.com; p. 16 Albie Venter/Shutterstock.com; p. 17 Gunter Ziesler/Peter Arnold/Getty Images; p. 21 Sam DCruz/Shutterstock.com.

Printed in the United States of America

CPSIA compliance information: Batch #CW14GS: For further information contact Gareth Stevens, New York, New York at 1-800-542-2595.

CONTENTS

Words in the glossary appear in **bold** type
the first time they are used in the text.

HYENA ATTACK!

A herd of **antelope** runs gracefully across the African **grassland** as the sun goes down. Suddenly, a large group of doglike creatures races after them. Hyenas! They're fast, and they're hungry.

One of the **vicious** predators runs into the middle of the herd. Antelope scramble in all directions to get away. Two more hyenas attack a slow young antelope and bring it down. The group fight over their weak prey as the rest of the antelope escape.

Fact Hunter

Hyenas look a bit like dogs, but they're actually more closely related to cats.

Hyenas may look cute at times, but they're vicious hunters!
▽

THREE KINDS

There are three kinds of hyenas: spotted, brown, and striped. The spotted hyena is the largest. All are omnivores, which means they eat meat, plants, and just about anything they can sink their teeth into!

Spotted hyenas live in central and southern Africa, while brown hyenas live mostly in southern Africa. Striped hyenas live in northern Africa and parts of the Middle East and Asia. All three like to live on grasslands, though some can be found in other **habitats** such as deserts, woodlands, and even mountains.

striped hyena

Because brown hyenas eat fruit, they can live in desert areas with few water sources.

spotted hyena

brown hyena

⚠ The three kinds of hyenas get their names from their fur coats.

ON THE HUNT

Hyenas are **scavengers**. They'll eat other animals' leftovers. They hunt as well. Besides antelope, hyenas eat all kinds of creatures, including **wildebeest**, snakes, birds, lizards, bugs, and even lions.

Brown hyenas and striped hyenas live in groups, but they hunt alone. Spotted hyenas live and hunt in large groups called clans. This means spotted hyenas can work together to bring down large prey. They usually attack weak, sick, or young animals of a herd.

Fact Hunter

A clan of spotted hyenas may have as many as 80 members!

Spotted hyenas are tricky hunters when they work together.
That's how they bring down prey larger than themselves.

"LAUGHING" HYENAS?

Have you ever heard the term "laughing hyena"? Spotted hyenas are sometimes called laughing hyenas because of the strange noises they make—a mix of laughing and gurgling. The hyenas don't make this sound because they think something is funny, though. They "laugh" when they're excited or on the hunt.

Striped hyenas don't make much noise, but they sometimes growl and roar when fighting other hyenas. Brown hyenas whine, squeal, and shriek if a predator approaches.

This spotted hyena's teeth remind us how dangerous these animals can be!

KILLER SENSES

Hyenas have some **adaptations** that help them hunt and scavenge. They have excellent eyesight. This is very useful at night, when hyenas are on the hunt. They also have a good sense of hearing. Hyenas can hear other predators on the hunt from miles away. They know they may be able to scavenge a meal if they follow the sounds.

Hyenas have a great sense of smell, too. They leave different scents, or smells, in their territory for other hyenas. Some scents tell their clan where they've looked for food. Certain scents tell other clans to stay away from their territory.

Each hyena has a special scent, so the group can tell one from another. ▼

13

HYENA CUBS

Most mother hyenas have one to four cubs at a time. Cubs have dark hair at first. They drink their mother's milk. It's hard being a hyena cub. They **compete** for food. Sometimes, brothers and sisters attack and kill each other!

After a time, hyena cubs begin to eat meat. If the mother hyena lives in a clan, she'll bring her cubs to the clan. The whole clan helps bring meat back to the cubs until they're old enough to hunt and take care of themselves.

Fact Hunter

Hyena cubs are born with teeth and ready to eat.

Female spotted hyenas stay with their clan for life, but males are forced out after a few years.

BONE CRUSHERS

Hyenas will eat anything, including hooves and bones! A full-grown hyena's teeth and jaws are so powerful that they can easily crush bones. A hyena has a tough stomach that can **digest** things other animals can't. They even eat body parts like horns and hair but later throw them up.

Hyenas don't have to kill to eat, and some, like the brown hyena, usually don't. Instead, they let other animals like lions do the hard work, and they eat the remains.

A large group of hyenas can scare lions away from their prey.

▽

HUNTED

Hyenas are fearsome, but they fear other animals. Their enemies include lions, wild dogs, and **jackals**. Other animals usually don't kill hyenas to eat them. They kill them because they compete for the same food sources. These animals usually attack when they find a hyena alone. This is another reason why living in groups is helpful to hyenas.

Different kinds of hyenas may attack each other. However, they tend to live in different habitats. Clans of hyenas may fight for territory and prey, too.

Fact Hunter

Hyena is spelled "hyaena" in many parts of the world.

Brown and striped hyenas can make their hair stand on end. It makes them look bigger than they really are.

CLEANUP CREW

Hyenas need to fear people, too. People kill hyenas to stop them from attacking livestock and eating crops. Hyenas usually avoid people, but, increasingly, people are moving into their habitat.

Hyenas aren't cuddly, and they'd make terrible pets. However, because they eat so many parts of dead animals, they clean up messes made by other animals. When hyenas hunt, they keep populations of animals in control. Hyenas play an important role in nature.

Just don't get too close!

Striped hyenas are now in danger of becoming **extinct**. ▶

Spotted Hyenas by the Numbers

length	34 to 59 inches (86 to 150 cm); tail, another 10 to 14 inches (25 to 36 cm)
height	28 to 35 inches (71 to 89 cm)
weight	90 to 190 pounds (41 to 86 kg)
life span	up to 25 years

21

GLOSSARY

adaptation: a change in an animal that makes it better able to live in its surroundings

antelope: an animal similar to a deer that lives in Africa and southwest Asia

compete: to try to win a struggle with others

digest: to break down food inside the body so that the body can use it

extinct: no longer living

grassland: land on which grass is the main kind of plant life

habitat: the natural place where an animal or plant lives

jackal: an African animal that looks like a bushy-tailed dog

scavenger: an animal that eats the remains of dead animals

vicious: dangerous and intending to do harm by fighting

wildebeest: another word for a gnu, an antelope that looks a bit like an ox with curved horns

FOR MORE INFORMATION

Books

Quinlan, Julia J. *Hyenas*. New York, NY: PowerKids Press, 2013.

Spilsbury, Louise. *Hyena*. Chicago, IL: Heinemann Library, 2011.

Websites

Brown Hyaena
www.arkive.org/brown-hyaena/hyaena-brunnea/
See amazing photos of the brown hyena.

Mammals: Spotted Hyena
sandiegozoo.org/animalbytes/t-spotted_hyena.html
Read much more about the spotted hyena.

Striped Hyena
animaldiversity.ummz.umich.edu/accounts/Hyaena_hyaena/
Find out how the striped hyena differs from the brown and the spotted hyena.

INDEX